Emotional I Mast

A Practical Guide

To Improving Your EQ

By Eric Jordan

TABLE OF CONTENTS

Chapter 1:

What Is Emotional Intelligence?

You might have heard that you should "develop" your EQ. That — in order to get ahead professionally, or master social situations — you have to "have good EQ". EQ, also known as emotional intelligence, is frequently mentioned in psychology and self-help literature, but what is it exactly? We might just as correctly call it emotional awareness, or emotional management skill, and it has the potential to entirely change your way of life.

Emotional intelligence has been a buzzword in the personal growth industry and in high-level corporate recruitment strategies since 1995, when Daniel Goleman used the term for his book title and topic. As we would say today, his use of it "went viral" immediately in the world of business and mental health. He abbreviates it as EI. You will also see it — as in this book — as EQ. The term was actually coined by two researchers, Peter Salavoy and John Mayer, co-authors of the 'Mayer-Salovey-Caruso Emotional intelligence test'.

EQ is the personal ability you have to recognize and label your own emotions and feelings. That's your starting point. You stop cold in the middle of a conversation you're having, for instance, and can say to yourself, "I was just feeling and expressing irritation and a mild degree of anger!"

Once you can recognize your own feelings to a degree of certainty, you will then move on to develop the ability to see emotions and feelings in others for what they are. If you can see feelings in yourself, you'll be able to identify them in others. That is the second step you would take if you are interested in developing your EQ – seeing others' feelings as they express them. As you are having a conversation with one or more other people, for instance, you have the thought, "John is feeling very enthusiastic about this. Peter is totally apathetic. Mary is irritated with the whole subject."

Those are the two aspects of the foundation of your EQ, your emotional intelligence. It's developing a habit of pausing and objectively asking yourself which feelings are in play at the moment, in yourself and in others.

The next level of emotional intelligence that you can develop for yourself is your personal ability to rein in or direct your emotions, to call on certain emotions, for instance, so that they help you perform better. Many of us understand that when we are experiencing strong anger and are explosively out-of-control, we cannot think clearly. If we cannot think clearly, we cannot make good decisions or act effectively.

Similarly, if we are experiencing a giddy exhilaration, it is hard for us to focus on any given task. Our exhilaration draws us back to the object of that feeling. We can't think of anything else. We then need to "calm down". The EQ ability to recognize and pull in this type of feeling allows us to return to clear-headedness. In ordinary conversation we might say, "She calmed herself down. He cheered himself up. They pulled themselves out of their depression." The ability to do that for yourself is called having high a EQ!

This third level of emotional intelligence is your personal ability to not only manage your own strong or expressed emotions, but to regulate them at will. This includes the ability to let go of, or even fully dissolve strong feelings – in the moment, at will. Related to this is your interpersonal ability to help others manage or regulate their own feelings, such as calming down a tearful child, or helping a person through a period of grief or mourning.

Consider this example:

A popular stage performer suffered excruciating stage fright. In the studio, she was relaxed and could sing with no holds barred. However, on stage with a live audience, she froze up. Her manager hooked her up with an EQ consultant. The consultant asked her how she felt just before going out on stage.

She said, "My muscles tighten up and get jumpy at the same time. My mouth goes dry. My heart starts to pound. I think about all of those people in the audience expecting great things from me and how loyal they have been to me over the years... and I freeze. I cannot walk another step towards the stage."

Her consultant then told her the story of another stage performer (she recognized his name) who had used the EQ consultant's services as well.

The consultant told her, "When I asked him how he felt just before going out on stage, guess what he said? He says his muscles tighten up and he gets jumpy. He says his mouth goes dry. He says his heart starts to pound. He says he thinks about all those great people who have been so loyal to him who are sitting out in the audience. And you know what? That gets him really excited to get out on that stage and start singing!"

He continued, "He is filled with the energy of what we call enthusiasm and courageousness. *You* feel the energy of fear and panic. Those energies are the same thing, just placed on flip side of the coin. The feeling of fear is the opposite of enthusiasm. Together we will see if we can't flip that coin right around..."

What the EQ consultant was going to teach the female stage performer was how to turn her feelings upside-down. And together, they succeeded. She gets a little flutter these days before going on the stage – yes, she admits to that – but mostly she's excited, enthusiastic and grateful for her loyal fan base.

That is the power and self-control of a high EQ individual!

When we say someone has high EQ, or good EQ, we mean that they are smart about emotions, and we tend to admire their emotional self-control and their ability to help others get back to a state of calm, too. We admire their ability to bounce back emotionally (1).

How is EQ different from IQ?

Emotional intelligence is our ability to identify, understand and manage or control our feelings. It is additionally our ability to perceive, understand and influence the emotions of other people.

There isn't really an EQ "score" or metric that states how "emotionally intelligent" you are. If a person is "EQ dumb", most people know it and will usually stay away. If an individual is "EQ smart", he or she acts like a magnet to people.

IQ is our "Intelligence Quotient". It is said to be one of the best ways to measure how brain-smart we are, with no regard to our emotional temperament. The IQ itself is actually a numerical score that is given upon testing, and has been around since the early 20th century (2). Our public schools have been trying to measure our intelligence quotients for decades. From about 10 or so IQ tests being used today, we know that the mean score is 100, and about two thirds of us score between IQ 85 and IQ 115; 5% of us score above 125 and 5% of us score below 75. One of the most known among the tests is the 'Stanford–Binet Intelligence Scales.'

Contrary to emotional intelligence, our personal IQ is commonly used to place us educationally, to assess any intellectual disabilities, to evaluate us when applying for specific job positions, and even to predict our degree of wealth or annual income over our lifetime.

IQ scores may gently rise as one gets older, if one continuously reads and learns new things (in other words, solicits the mind continuously). In all cases, the IQ score is only a reflection of "how smart you are at the moment of testing." Contrary to emotional intelligence, we have come to believe that our intellectual capabilities are statistically measurable. Whether that is actually true or not is up for debate, however, due to the strong influence high EQ can have on one's overall intelligence!

The World of Work, Leadership and EQ

Are there actually professions where high emotional intelligence is needed? Yes, numerous ones, in face, and the hiring managers of all sizes and types of businesses are looking for people with a developed EQ! Let's look at why that is the case.

When is the last time someone tried to sell you something? Ah, sales people... The best ones know all about emotional buying. They know which buttons to push, as it were, to stir up your urgent lust, craving and desire to have the particular widget or gadget they are promoting. They may not even formally learn EQ skills, but the best intuitive sales people master it nonetheless.

"When L'Oréal started hiring sales people based on emotional competency, the high EQ reps outsold the traditionally chosen ones by over $90,000 [annually]." (3)

Century-old personal care product company L'Oréal is one of hundreds of major corporations (add Google, AT&T, U.S. Air Force and 75 percent of "Fortune 500" companies) that ask their sales people, managers and leaders to come in to the job with high emotional intelligence.

Notably, the internet giant Google has lightened up on its college degree requirement, realizing that a high grade-point-average only indicates what it measures: strong IQ and potential for academic success. In other words, only the graduate's brain smarts, not necessarily his street smarts, innovative talent or EQ. They now seek other types of intelligence as well. The bottom line? The use of more emotional awareness, self-control, empathy and relationship management skills kicks up sales – whether the EQ comes from salespeople, managers or executives. High EQ in the company is the real deal for results (4).

The acting profession is an excellent one from which to look at EQ. Like many professions, it is both an art and a science. Have you occasionally noticed an actor's flat performance in a film or stage play? That, of course, can be for any number of reasons. However, if that actor does not have high emotional intelligence, they cannot portray a range of feelings convincingly.

Remember that EQ is defined as an individual's ability to identify, evaluate, control, and express feelings. What do actors do if not express feelings? Our most beloved performers are good at communicating the feelings to us through their portrayal of a character who is part of a greater story. Those that have the highest emotional intelligence, in combination with a mastery of the art and science of acting, are the performers we love the most.

Mental health workers receive EQ training as part of their knowledge base and toolkit. Therapists like psychiatrists and psychologists are very in tune with the role a patient's feelings are playing in their health and wellness, as well as the part played by emotions in illnesses like chronic depression, destructive addictive behaviors, eating disorders, anxiety issues and others. In fact, notice how often the diagnosis actually names the feeling!

EQ is not only a tool for these professionals in diagnostics, but in relating to and gaining rapport with their patients more effectively during face-to-face therapy sessions. Empathy *can* be learned, and the most successful mental health professionals typically excel in this area.

Business-world managers and leaders of people who have a high EQ readily understand, empathize, and connect with the people around them. The emotionally developed leader easily develops instant rapport with a stranger, and goes on to develop an excellent working relationship with them. This helps get the best job performance and teamwork from the individual.

Hundreds of studies over the past 2 to 3 decades have cemented the power of high emotional intelligence in the workplace. As an example, studies comparing outstanding managers with average ones found that the differences were all in the degree of EQ of the manager. Strong EQ rocketed managers to a recognized level of excellence. This goes beyond traditional leadership skills and knowledge development.

A corporate study at PepsiCo determined that strong Emotional intelligence skills helped managers exceed yearly revenue goals by 15 to 20%. Interestingly, weak EQ skills led managers to underperform by the same percentage range.

A study of PhD's spanning 40 years at the University of California at Berkeley concluded that well-developed EQ was four times more powerful than strong IQ in predicting who succeeded in their chosen field.

The a highly developed EQ allows a leader to truly perform in the workplace. There are different types of problems that can be addressed, solved or resolved from the perspective of high emotional intelligence. Your average data-driven, low-EQ manager cannot get any traction in these types of issues.

Consider these three examples:

1.

How can you get your team to work at a higher level of performance and goal achievement? The use of inspirational storytelling and company ritual can inspire your team members to rise to a new level of performance. This solution comes from emotions.

2.

How can you energize your people when the going gets rough or when your business is threatened by outside factors? You demonstrate your certainty through your own positive emotional state, your expressions of confidence in them, and your trust in them and belief in their skillsets. You have their back, feel for them and with them, and literally roll up your sleeves at their side – this expresses a high degree of engagement with them through a visible expression of emotional support.

3.

Companies want emotionally intelligent leaders, as it has been proven time and again that employees with such leaders are about four times less likely to leave the company. What company isn't seeking to reduce costly staff turnover? Employees also stay because of the rapport and relationship the manager develops with them, and because a high EQ leader is a higher-level achiever. And what employee does not want to be on a high-performing, top-achieving team?

Have you noticed something? A pattern perhaps? <u>Rapport</u> and <u>relationship</u> are about interacting successfully with people – a good trait to have if you have a leadership role, a medical one or any interactive part you play in any team or team-created outcome (5).

Real Life High-EQ Leaders

In large corporations, the many layers of managers and team-leaders are normally hidden from public awareness, and we don't really know who those EQ-successful individuals are. Instead, we mostly hear about those corporations' CEOs, so let's take a look at which corporate CEOs are known for their high levels of emotional intelligence.

On the one hand, this is a highly subjective list of people, so bear that in mind as you read on — on the other hand, the success of their corporations lends credence to their EQ capabilities. The data-driven bottom line doesn't lie about success or failure.

1.

He has a quirky laugh and self-deprecating smooth style. He is quick to move from getting into the minds of his customers to getting into their hearts, using relationship as a business strategy. [Jeff Bezos, Amazon.com]

2.

He says you can do the same work he does even with a lower IQ. It's all about controlling your "emotional urges" as you navigate the financial markets! [Warren Buffett, Berkshire Hathaway Investments]

3.

He is disciplined and self-aware, and his deeply loyal team are in awe of his listening ability. [John Donahoe, eBay]

4.

This leader does MBWA (Management By Wandering Around), so everyone gets to build a relationship with him. His people thrive on his handwritten notes to them, praising a job well done. His focus and attention on the individual during any conversation with him is legendary. [Alan Mulally, Ford Motor Company]

5.

She acts just like one of us. She wanders the halls barefoot or singing a song. She helps employees see that they don't have "a job", but they are responding to a calling. [Indra Nooyi, PepsiCo]

If you are a history buff, you have probably heard about the former English prime minister Winston Churchill's leadership style, which has been extensively studied through the years. Most would agree that he was a charismatic leader, who kept his citizens looking up, looking forward and staying positive — primarily through his highly inspirational speeches during WWII. During those dark times he was the very model of strength and courage to the people of the United Kingdom.

From more recent history, there is the former so-called "Meditating President" of Mozambique in Africa, Joaquim Chissano. He practiced what is known as transcendental meditation (TM), and upon election required the people working with him in government to learn the activity as well. Imagine a major corporation or a major government actually paying its leadership and officials to learn how to meditate! That is just what he did. Under Chissano's leadership, which lasted from 1986 to 2005, the whole personnel of government, the armed forces and police of Mozambique were required to practice TM twice daily.

This practice was actually begun in 1994, and the emotional awareness that grew from it was astonishing in its impacts. The results? The 15-year civil war ended, and the country was returned to peace, and the rebuilding of its prosperity began (6).

Personal Relationships and EQ

When you have a well-developed, highly functioning EQ, it shows in all aspects of your life. It certainly helps you stand out in the work world, but it also makes you remarkable in relationships with family, friends and strangers. For others, it is perhaps the lack of EQ that makes them stand out.

Here's a few signs that you have a rather low EQ:

1.

You have a hard time breaking away from your digital screen (phone, computer etc.) and thus don't know how to really create a face-to-face relationship.

2.

You are not good at all at making and sustaining eye contact – and even avoid it.

3.

You are well-known for your inappropriate responses to circumstances. For instance, you spontaneously burst out in laughter when someone near you falls and injures himself or even bleeds, or when you see someone nearby in a fit of anger who is yelling and flailing around.

4.

You always seem to rub people the wrong way; you irritate people. In other words, you don't know how to get along with people – it's not intuitive for you to know how to act, what to say and especially how to say it.

5.

You are a "me first" kind of person. You open a door to go through it yourself – you never hold it for someone else. Slowing down to help others is not something you truly understand, or ever do.

6.

You wear out your welcome. You're the one who closes the bar, or whom a host puts out with the cat because the party ended long ago and he wants to go to bed.

7.

You are truthful and blunt to a fault. You make others cringe, cry ... and distrust you.

Some signs that you have a <u>high emotional intelligence</u>?

1.

When you meet new people, you're curious to find out all about them, who they are and so on. You are not shy in asking them for that information. And what is more, you know how to ask those questions in such a friendly, comfortable way that you indeed get willing responses.

2.

You are well-known for just clicking with people. You seem to have instant rapport with almost everyone.

3.

When you are upset, you can put your finger on exactly why that is the case. You are not confused by emotional highs and lows throughout a normal day. You handle them because you know yourself (in other words, you are self-aware).

4.

You are a pretty good listener and have good focus! This means that you can also skillfully manage distractions and interruptions, so that you don't hurt anyone's feelings.

5.

You simply "get" when it is the right time to leave a particular gathering; Not offending anyone by leaving too early or, in other cases, overstaying your welcome.

In short? EQ is from the heart. IQ is from the brain. And humans live from both! Next, we'll take a closer look at exactly *how* you can improve your EQ...

Chapter 2:

How to Improve Your Emotional Intelligence: By Yourself

While improving one's IQ may be a bit confusing, there are some very simple and easily applicable ways to improve your EQ. These exercises and techniques will give you results fairly quickly – if you practice them regularly. The changes that they bring will be easy for you to discern, and as you practice them others will start noticing the difference in you as well.

Exercise 1: Pay Attention!

The most basic exercise you can do, and a great way to start off your EQ training, is to simply start ***paying attention***. Your objective is not, for now, to change how you feel, but simply to _observe_ your emotions and feelings as they emerge.

For maximum effectiveness, do this for 7 consecutive days:

1.

    Get a pocket-sized notebook, or simply staple a couple of sheets of paper together and fold them into your pocket.

2.

Pick an hour each day during which you will be observing the emotions and feelings you experience personally. Don't bother with other people's feelings at this time.

3.

As you observe yourself experiencing a feeling, pull out your notebook and jot down the _exact word describing the feeling_. Don't edit. Don't overanalyze. Don't try to change the feeling you're having because you're feeling bad about it. Just write it down and put your notebook back in your pocket. If you feel the emotion again – or many other times – during the hour-long exercise, write it down at each separate experience of it.

4.

Keep a running list for the hour that day. Don't continue with the exercise when the hour is up. Just go about your business as usual.

Do this same thing again the next day, but during a different hour of the day. This way you'll be able to observe yourself morning, noon and night. Note all the feelings you experience in a running list.

Exercise 2: Emotional Analysis

Part A:

Color-coding your list is a very useful tool for seeing _patterns_. Using different colored highlighting markers or pencils will help you do this analysis with ease.

1.

After a week of doing the first exercise, pull out your notebook to look at the list of emotions and feelings that you've written down. Choose a certain color, and highlight the single most frequently recurring feeling that you experienced the past week. Highlight all instances of that particular feeling in your list with that color.

2.

With a different color marker, find another frequent feeling you have experienced and highlight the word everywhere it appears in the list.

3.

Keep highlighting and color-coding your other feelings until all of them are covered.

4.

See which ones are "orphans", that is, appearing only one, two or three times that week.

5.

Take a good look at your analysis. At the bottom of your list, write the top four feelings you experienced that week.

Part B:

Now, we'll look closer at each of the four feelings which you most frequently experienced:

1.

Examine whether you define them as positive or negative feelings.

2.

Try to remember when you experienced those feelings.

3.

Recall what triggered you having that particular emotion. Make a small note of the reason or trigger.

4.

Was having that feeling at that time beneficial or detrimental to the current circumstances?

5.

Could things have gone better if you had had different feelings at the time?

6.

What are your thoughts about having had those feelings? Just write down everything that comes to mind without judging it.

7.

Think back on three or four events of the past week. Could you have expressed a different feeling or would that have been impossible for you at the time? Be honest. We are only observing, not expecting change right now!

8.

Can you accept that you had those feelings – and not beat yourself up about it, yes or no?

9.

Would it be advantageous to rein in or dissolve one or more of those four feelings? Advantageous to whom? How? Write your answers down.

If you have gone through all the steps of these two exercises, well done! You have now engaged in some deep and meaningful self-reflection.

Remember: Knowing the self is the first step towards real, effective, long-term change!

Exercise 3: Learning To Read The Body

Almost all of your heavier, negative emotions as well as your lighter, positive feelings can easily be felt as sensations in your physical body.

Consider the feeling of anger. What happens in your body when you are feeling quite angry? Your muscles tighten up – fists clenched, muscles taut and ready for attack, face all tied up in an angry grimace. And then there is your voice, also a natural part of your body. Depending on your style of anger, your voice will get very tight and quiet or very loose and loud. It doesn't take many experiences of anger for you to identify that feeling from how your body is reacting.

Now consider the feeling of sadness or grief. Your body also manifests this feeling. It becomes heavy, like you're carrying around a ton of cement, making you feel like you're being pulled downwards (thus the metaphor of "feeling down"). If you are sitting, it's hard for you to get up; if you are standing, it's hard for you to walk. You just don't want to move.

Depending on the degree of sadness or grief, and how sudden it has come upon you, your eyes might start to tear up or sob uncontrollably. If the sadness is particularly serious, you may even feel like curling up in your bed and going to sleep. The effects on the physical are indeed easy to recognize for most of us.

Let us now consider a lighter, happier feeling that we call enthusiasm. This makes us feel great! Your body feels brilliant, light and full of energy. Your voice may sound brighter and more inspiring; your speech will speed up. Your eyes shine. Your face is stretched with a big smile, and perhaps bubbly laughter may even pour out of you at times. All of this is happening in your body. You can feel it!

Decisions

Once you have become more proficient at identifying your feelings, analyzing them for patterns and tendencies, and also watching your own body language for feelings – are you emotionally intelligent? Are you done?

There is good news and there is bad news. The good news is that, by taking action with the aforementioned exercises, you know how to pay attention to your feelings better than most people do. The bad news is that you haven't yet learned how to rein in the effects of "unwanted" feelings! **All** high-EQ people can do this at will. Another piece of good news is that <u>you can teach yourself to do this</u>.

Start now by practicing on *deciding* how to react to your emotions. You may not be able to choose what emotions to feel, but you *can* decide what to do with them. One of the common mental traps you can fall into (even smart people do this) is to rationalize a feeling by telling yourself "Everyone has this feeling from time to time. It's only human!" It may sound reasonable, but it's not necessarily true!

For now, though, when you experience a strong emotion, you have a decision to make;

You can:

> - Recognize the feeling and let it happen, because it will eventually wear itself out, OR

> - Recognize the feeling and control it consciously right away, before it affects your actions.

This is where "feeling with the body" can be useful.

Exercise 4: Feel & Release

Remember that we asked this question in part A of exercise number 2:

"Would it be advantageous to rein in or dissolve one or more of those four feelings?"

For your learning purposes now, think about a feeling where your answer was a clear 'Yes!'. There is actually a very simple way to dissolve any feeling that arises and is noticeable in the body. Mental health professionals have been using and teaching it for decades, as part of their toolkit for helping emotionally overwhelmed patients. On average, it takes less than 2 minutes! Here's how it is done:

(Do this whenever you notice a feeling that has already arisen and gripped your body in some way).

1.

Notice where the feeling has collected into a hardened ball of energy, so to speak. It may seem that it has grabbed you by the throat, tightened up your chest area, or formed a hard clenching in your gut area. Take notice of where the feeling has collected.

2.

Now, also notice that you have had this bodily sensation before; It was just a feeling! Now that you know this, you are in charge of it. You are its boss. *You* are the master of *you*.

3.

Close your eyes. Bring your inner attention and awareness to that hardened ball of energy – that grabbing, tight or clutching feeling. Simply imagine that you are opening the door in front of that tight feeling. Why are you opening the door? You are inviting that tight energy to leave!

4.

It is a mental image, a visualization, that you create here. Silently talk to that clenching energy. Say, "The door is open. I let you go. Please leave through the open door." Keep repeating those phrases five times.

5.

With your mind's eye, you are simultaneously watching as this energy leaves through the open door. You may actually see an image of this happening – maybe dark smoke billows out the doorway, for instance. You may see nothing at all, and that is fine too.

6.

Notice how your body relaxes as the release unfolds. Where the feeling had grabbed your body in a feeling of tightness, you are now feeling more relaxed. Now, consciously allow your body to relax.

7.

Do you still feel some of that feeling in your body? If you still feel it, simply keep the door open and continue to invite the feeling to leave.

8.

You can name the feeling as you talk to it. "Fear, I invite you to leave through this open door." Or you can just call it an energy that needs to leave: "I let you go, energy. You have no place here. Please leave through the open door." Adjust the process to be most applicable to your personal symbolism.

9.

Your goal is to continue this open-door releasing until your body tells you the feeling is gone, or that the energy tightness is fully relaxed.

What have you just done? You have released that feeling! You have mastered it. You have commanded it to do something – and it has followed your command. All of us really have this much power over our emotions! Recognize, accept, release. It really is that simple.

Emotionally Charged Thinking

With a bit of reflection, we realize that feelings fill our thoughts as well. While we have some neutral (or "objective") thoughts, most of our thinking is actually charged with either positive or negative emotions.

Even the simplest thought — like, "I'm running late" — can be full of emotions. It may be accompanied by anxiety, apathy, fear, self-importance, acceptance, joyful excitement and so on. The feeling that arises with the thought can be positive or negative, depending on the context.

Look at the following examples and consider whether the thought comes from — or is filled with — positive or negative feelings, or if it's more objective and neutral.

- The sun is shining.

- She is in a crappy mood, watch out!

- What is wrong with them today?

- How dare you!

- How does he do that?

- I woke up feeling so great today!

- And to think I woke up feeling good...

- How could you be so stupid!

- Is it smart to do it this way, do you think?

- It's raining.

- Look at how well I did the job!

- Piss off! Get away from me!

- I'll never, ever, get it right.

Keep in mind that the statement's feelings may shift depending on the mood of the person who verbalizes them. Think of how actors are capable of changing emphasis on one word or infusing a certain statement with emotion. This skill is especially vital to have as a voice actor; Such an actor must convey real meaning through their voice alone. With some training, any high-EQ individual can easily learn to do this as well!

Exercise 5: Learning to Avoid Thought Traps

In your path towards higher EQ, you will most likely run into "thought traps" — which tend to become habitual for many of us. A typical thought trap usually unfolds something like this:

1.

You have a negative thought – perhaps in reaction to something another person said or did to you.

2.

You repeat that thought over and over, almost obsessively, in your head.

3.

You come to believe that this thought is true about that person – or about you.

OR

You stir up negative feelings in yourself all on your own – because no one else has the power to do so, right? – and start feeling them in your body through a tightness in your throat, chest or gut area.

We all have lots and lots of self-talk going on throughout the day – those inner conversations that go on in that space between our ears. And, unfortunately — for the vast majority of us — it is mostly negative! We talk ourselves into and out of doing things, learning more, changing habits and so on through *negative self-talk*. Because the negative talk is usually more prevalent than the positive, it is not always so easy to make positive changes in our lives.

Call it negative self-talk. Call it a negative thought trap. Can you see how such a thinking pattern is going to be habitual in *low-EQ individuals*? A high EQ person would instantly see the reaction for what it is, accept it, and let it go. Consequently, they'd move up into a higher emotional state, where they would experience plenty of energy and more positive thoughts.

Look at the patterns you've identified about yourself from your prior exercises. Do you have any thought traps mentioned in your notes? Look for something similar to this:

Immediate negative judgement of others ("What's wrong with him/her", "That is so stupid").

Or

Taking offense ("What? He *insulted* me! The bastard!", "How dare she make such a statement about my clothing when she's always a mess herself!")

Part A:

Similar to what we did in the first exercise, we need to develop an awareness of when we are having negative thoughts. Do this:

Every ten minutes for the next hour, stop. Stop everything you are doing and ask yourself "What is the predominant thought I have just been thinking?" Write down the complete thought. Don't do anything about it yet, just write it down.

At the end of the hour, you will have written down six thoughts.

1.

Do any of the thoughts repeat themselves?

2.

How many of the thoughts are positive and how many are negative?

The next day, try to do this exercise every ten minutes for 30 to 60 minutes, but do it while you are in conversation or meetings with other individuals. Quietly jot down the thoughts that you identify.

Later, ask these questions about those thoughts:

1.

How many of the thoughts are charged with negative feelings and emotions, or negative judgements?

2.

How many of the thoughts are charged with positive feelings and emotions, or express admiration, accolades and appreciation of someone — in other words, positive judgements?

Remember that your objective in doing this exercise in two situations is to develop your awareness of the nature and quality of your thinking. That's all. For the moment you're not doing anything else.

Part B:

Do this exercise when you are alone in fairly quiet surroundings. Mental health professionals also use this tool to help their patients calm their minds, just as they use the prior feel-and-release process to help them calm their bodies.

1.

Notice when you are spinning in your head around a single topic, or having a recurring thought that you just can't let go of.

2.

Once you have noticed which thought keeps popping up or that you are spinning in your head, stop! Stop and ask yourself this question:

"Could I let go of listening to my mind, yes or no?"

Naturally, for these purposes, you want to answer yes. Once you have said "Yes!" out loud or in silence, immediately repeat the question again and answer "Yes" once again. Ask and answer over and over again. After a minute or so, you'll notice that the mental spinning has stopped and your mind is quieter.

Of course, the mind stays quiet only for a moment or two, but that is long enough for you to gather in your personal power again, right? It's long enough for you to move back into more positive emotions and thoughts.

Self-Management

Self-management — in regards to improving your EQ — takes awareness of your own feelings, behaviors and reactions one step further. Self-management is your at-will ability to delay personal gratification, in the name of more personal mastery over strong feelings or urges. In the name of a quiet, more balanced observation of other people around you. In the name of allowing others to shine.

Let's say, for instance, that you always cave in to your craving to eat chocolate whenever it is available. Typically, you'll have a thought flash through your head that says, "I want chocolate RIGHT NOW!" And you will grab some chocolate and eat it without further delay. You might ask what eating chocolate has to do with high EQ. It's not the chocolate that's at issue here, but the *feeling* of "craving" it. Part of what successful portion control or food choice is all about is *delaying gratification.*

Anyone who has been on one or more diets realizes this! That is, you do not cave into that strong feeling of desire for the thing. You put things off, or delay them, at least for a bit. You bite your tongue, you feel that feeling of lust and craving rising up in your body. You just feel it. You recognize it, and you let it go in the way which we have gone through in the previous pages.

Just these few steps, which may last only a minute or two, help you self-manage that feeling of desire for the chocolate, by delaying impulsive action. If you are relentless and determined about the chocolate, you continue to delay gratification until the entire feeling of lust for chocolate is permanently eliminated.

As another example, let's say, for instance, that from a feeling of superiority (a feeling that falls in the category of pride and judgement), when it comes to starting a new project at the office, or doing a family project at home with the children, you just cannot help yourself from controlling exactly how things unfold. You cannot keep yourself from telling every participant in the project how to do their part of the work.

What is more, you tell them how to do it in the detail. And beyond that? You're always looking over their shoulders to make sure they are they are doing it exactly according to your prescription. No beloved leader of high EQ micro-manages his people like this! So what do you need to do to move out of this low-EQ tendency to reign supreme over everyone else? You need to **delay your gratification**.

Sure, you may be highly gratified by the feeling of superiority. In much the same way as with a craving for chocolate, you will need to bite your tongue whenever you wish to tell someone that they're doing things wrong. Instead, you'll ask them their opinion on how things are progressing. This will certainly be a challenge to begin with if you're a classic "know-it-all" (and that's why this exercise is so useful!) as you break an old habit in order to rise into greater EQ.

At every opportunity to jump in and correct someone's mistake, you instead take the opportunity to bite your tongue and ask the individual, "How are things going?" Listen attentively to the responses you receive. Again, stop yourself whenever you want to tell them how wrong they are, or how inefficient they are, or in any other way want to assert your superiority, real or imagined.

Your goal here is to step back and allow others to shine — after all, everyone wants to shine as their leader looks on! Your goal here is to consider the possibility that other people may also know as much as you do, and are as smart as you are. Your goal here is to — with the use of emotional intelligence — develop more harmonious interactions with the people around you.

Next, we'll see how EQ depends closely on a thing called...

Chapter 3:

Mindfulness

The concept of mindfulness comes to us from the Eastern cultures, and particularly from Buddhism — concepts that are over 2,500 years old. Its simple objective is to take you into a dynamic focus and lead you to fully paying attention. You pay attention to what is going on around you, to which emotions you are feeling, to how and what you are saying to others, to how and what you are thinking silently within your own mind, to how you are acting and behaving out in the world either alone or amongst others.

See how this ties into developing your EQ? It's great!

In our Western societies, mindfulness courses and classes have mushroomed only over the past four decades or so. Mindfulness is now a mainstream concept and practice in Europe and North America. In fact, it's not far off track to say that many Westerners eased into full meditation practice through the doorway of mindfulness practice.

The Western medical and mental health communities, at the same time, came to adapt Eastern mindfulness practices and approaches to their own needs; They have indeed been shown over time to help patients who have mental and emotional health issues. The mindfulness practices help calm those patients so that they can better benefit from the professionals' advice and further therapy. Western psychology and psychiatry have also devised some more "Westerner-friendly" ways of learning and practicing mindfulness.; Medical professionals have assisted their patients in becoming more mindful, and seen it notably help reduce symptoms of depression, stress and anxiety, among others.

Versions of mindfulness and EQ that we see in these pages have also been extremely useful in diminishing or fully eliminating emotional trauma. Trauma from wartime experiences, from childhood or adult physical abuse or violence result in negative, protective feelings moving into place in our psyche.

Whether it manifests as recurring nightmares or sleepless nights *in fear* of terrible nightmares, a strong anxiety around certain personality types, or a panicky retreat from society altogether – such strong feelings and emotions associated with trauma can be released through mindfulness practice.

Knowing how to let go of the feelings helps diminish the power of the related memory as well. Military personnel returning from war zones and benefiting from a mindful release of traumatic feelings have gone so far as to state, "I finally got my life back".

The Essence of Mindfulness

Determination. Awareness. Attention.

These are three key words that help you understand what mindfulness is.

Mindfulness means <u>deliberately paying attention</u>. Intentionally focusing. Nonjudgmentally observing life and living as it occurs around you. Being aware of your surroundings through all your senses. If you are not paying attention, you don't know whether you are missing out on something that matters to you! You can only decide what matters to you by giving attention to everything, and then prioritizing.

Mindfulness is a useful state from which to observe what's going on within self, within other people, and out in the world at large. You pay attention to:

- What is going on around you.

- Which emotions you are experiencing.

- How you are talking to people and what you are saying.

- How people are talking to you and what they are saying.

- Body language – yours and others'.

- What others are doing and what they need.

- How and what you are thinking.

- How, how much and what you eat and drink and take into the body.

- Nature – sounds, colors and movement.

- And much more!

In other words, mindfulness is a dynamic state of awareness. It is a lively, conscious way of registering and processing information. This awareness of what is going on from moment to moment occurs without any judgement on your part.

We have all noticed young children engrossed in a given task. Nothing can pull their attention from it. They are creating some form of art, or building something, or they're lost in a beloved story that they know by heart. We as adults can go into "the zone", too! We are similarly experiencing a mindful absorption in the activity we are performing: running a long distance, reading an engrossing novel, lost in kneading the bread dough. Nearly no interference, noise or interruption seems to be able to break our focus. As the saying goes, "wild horses couldn't pull us away."

Millennia-old religious and spiritual practices have used some type of mindfulness technique from their very beginnings. Rites often blended them into practices. Prayer, singing hymns or chanting are nothing more than means of focusing – being mindful – on the spiritual energy and connection with the divine. Meditation (and mindfulness is part of achieving that quiet mind) is a spiritual aspect of many religions, including the Baha'i faith, Buddhism, Daoism, Hinduism, Jainism and Sikhism. By practicing mindfulness as we present it here, you are joining centuries of practitioners.

That being said, sustained mindfulness is a tall order for most people! It means you have to pause and pay attention to absolutely everything going on around you and within you. That's a lot to ask of anyone caught in the hustle-bustle of modern life. It's a lot to ask as we are traveling, running businesses and earning a living, raising families, managing our homes.

Being mindful is difficult for the busy person that you are, granted. Especially with our last two or three decades of increasing solicitation by technology, media and the devices we all carry around to communicate, it's hard to let go of that (apparent) connection and just observe attentively with our five senses for a while. We just don't like to stop! But stop is exactly what we must do if we are to practice mindfulness and reap the benefits of doing so.

Becoming mindful means that most of us have to learn brand-new habits. Anyone can develop a more mindful state of being. Indeed, throughout the centuries, a number of specific activities have helped humans become fully aware and stay in the moment: Yoga, many martial arts such as Aikido, Chi Gong or Tai Chi, and meditation are some of the ancient ways we have moved ourselves into mindfulness. The ancients who lived with attention and determination were able to move into deeper, more sustained and long-term mindful states, as they quieted the noise of the ordinary mind and observed the world from a more peaceful state (7).

15th century poet Kabir said,

"Wherever you are, that is the entry point."

That is an important comment to keep in mind, because the first-time practitioner of mindfulness (and meditation as a whole) will get frustrated by wondering where to start.

Exercise 1: Learning the Basics

The purpose of mindfulness is to draw your mind away from the noise of thinking about the past and future. Mindfulness draws you into the present moment, into the *now*. So, as Kabir said, wherever you are *right now* is your entry point into mindfulness. Let's look at what that means for your first session of mindfulness practice:

1.

Notice how you are feeling right now, in a general way, and

see if you have any judgements about that.

2.

Notice how you're feeling in your body:

If your body is fidgety, and revolting against sitting still, just allow yourself to feel fidgety! That's fine. That is where you are right now. That fidgety feeling is your entry point into your mindfulness session.

3.

Notice how you're feeling in your mind:

If your mind is wandering, thinking about what to have for dinner tonight or other such distractions, that's fine! That's where you are right now. Your mind is wandering in the future. Your mind is wandering in the past. Allow it to be acceptable that your mind is wandering... just for now. In other words, start by sitting as quietly in body and in mind as you can, at this particular moment.

4.

Next, you take a conscious decision to focus. You let go of everything going on around you – pressing matters on your agenda, a to-do list that never ends, wanting to get back on the internet. Decide to let go of all outside concerns for the 5 or 15 minutes of your mindfulness practice right now. You can do this!

5.

Now sit or stretch out – there is no rule about your body's position as long as you are comfortable and relaxed.

6.

Now is when you start to pay closer attention to your body and its tensions. You will consciously command tense muscles to relax, and then you just watch as they obey your command!

7.

Start now to notice your body's gentle breath in and out.

8.

Notice the temperature of the air all around you.

9.

Listen to the variety of sounds that are in your space – birdsong, the refrigerator motor, automobile traffic and so on. Simply take notice, and then move on.

10.

Take a few deep breaths and relax your muscles again.

That's it for now!

Please note that your entire mindfulness session can be you, using your senses in just this way:

1. Muscle relaxation.

2. Body's breath in and out.

3. The feel of the ambient air temperature on your skin.

4. Nearby sounds.

After all, how often is it that you decide simply to focus on what your five senses perceive in the moment?

Be mindful – attentive and conscious – in your first practice sessions of what your five senses are capable of telling you. Challenge yourself to notice more and more sounds, to feel a range of sensations on your skin or in your nostrils, to smell pleasant and unpleasant odors, to notice relaxed and tense muscles.

Exercise 2: Food Connection

In our societies' haste to fill all of our waking hours with activity and things that must get done, one of our age-old traditions has gotten lost. That tradition is mindfulness about our meals, eating and food in general.

If you are also one of those people whose lifestyle has pushed quiet, relaxed meals off your daily schedule, use the following mindfulness practice to become more conscious of what you eat, how you eat and how much you eat. Becoming more mindful of these aspects of eating will also relax your body so that it can process the food you give it more efficiently!

This is an exercise that you will do primarily while actually eating and chewing your food:

1.

Sit with your bowl or plate of prepared food in front of you. With your hands in your lap, gaze at the food and become aware of its colors and textures. You are using your eyes for this mindfulness.

2.

Lean into the food enough so that you can start to smell the fragrances wafting off of the plate. Do this with your eyes closed. You have seen and identified the foods on your plate, but smell the food now with your eyes closed. Do the fragrances correspond with the food you have identified? Become mindful of whether this is or is not so.

3.

Take a bite of one type of food. Let the food sit on your tongue without chewing it yet. Ask your body this question:

"Do you want this food?"

4.

Typically, your body will respond with some kind of energy movement. Just notice whether the energy is pleasant or unpleasant. In other words, is the energy saying, "Yes, I want it" or "No, I do not"? Make note of the answer. If it is No – what do you decide to do?

5.

Then, chew your food. Be mindful of the number of times you chew. This is not in order to follow a rule about chewing! It is for you to become aware of how long you actually keep a mouthful of food in your mouth. It is also for you to become mindful of the flavors exploding on your tongue – or the food's subtler flavor and textures.

Doing this entire exercise has helped many people gently and effortlessly lose weight! Taking your time helps you eat less and enjoy more. When your body says, "No more" – listen. Stop eating.

Other Applications

Use your imagination and look for moments during your ordinary day to practice mindfulness. Look for times during your day when you can focus your five senses into more mindfulness. Pay attention to the actual activity (standing, driving, sitting, eating), the people around you, the environment surrounding you and so on. Here are some examples of when you might do a mindfulness exercise:

- Driving a vehicle.

- Riding the train or the bus.

- Standing in line waiting for something.

- Preparing food in your own kitchen.

- Standing in the shower.

- Sitting in a meeting.

Benefits of Mindfulness

There are many levels of benefits to the practice of mindfulness:

Biologically, practice of mindfulness has been proven to increase telomerase (the caps at the end of our genes), with an effect of reducing cell damage in our body. Less cell damage leads to a longer life. Mindfulness also strengthens our immune system, which allows our body to more effortlessly fight off diseases ranging from the common cold to life-threatening conditions like cancer.

Emotionally, mindfulness and the focus it requires pulls us out of our hard or strong feelings into a more neutral, quieter space. We are thus calmer. We experience less stress. It is easier for us to stay in a happy or peaceful mood.

Mentally, the intention to silently observe gently leads our minds to quiet down. When our minds are still, our concentration on our point of focus can increase. Our mental acuity – the sense of mental sharpness – is improved. We may develop a better relationship with food, for example, and thus break our mental pattern of "beating ourselves up". Relationally, we are happier in family and other relationships, because we are in a quiet state of harmony with our environment and the people who surround us.

If you have been applying what we have gone through so far, you've engaged in some serious self-reflection, but what about other people? Let's see now how we can better decipher where other people are coming from. Let's see how we can better connect with them based on your new and improved awareness.

Chapter 4:

How To Improve Your Emotional Intelligence: With Others

Once you have had some active practice observing your own feelings and emotions, you can then start observing those of other people as well. There are numerous simple exercises to help you improve in this area, but one absolutely vital skill should grab your focus day in and day out as you become more emotionally intelligent.

Most people on the planet enjoy one particular sound above and beyond all others. That is the sound of their name, pronounced correctly and with respect! People with somewhat odd names might get a bit more frustrated than Mary, Robert and John about this. It takes more attentive listening to the unusual pronunciation of some names to get them right...and then to remember them hours or months later.

And it's in attentive and active listening that high-EQ individuals rise head and shoulders above the crowd. Not just for getting the names of people right every time, but also in intently listening and watching for information and data which is not communicated with actual spoken words. High-EQ individuals not only listen to everyone's words, but also to everyone's body language.

As we've touched on before, body language communicates either supportive or contradictory information to the words coming out of your mouth. Body language speaks to our visual senses, and educators have long understood that most students actually achieve about 60% of their learning through their eyes.

Emotional intelligence means being aware that feelings drive both our best and our worst behaviors. For some of us who are more natural observers than others, we readily recognize this in other people. Most of us need to train ourselves to observe and understand. Active listening helps.

The best novelists and screenplay writers are active and attentive observers of humankind. They have to be, as understanding the role of emotions is how they develop the characters depicted in their stories. At the end of the fast-moving action thriller novel, for instance, you may say to yourself that the hero of the story really was an adrenaline junkie; he was always taking big risks that defied rationality and reason. He felt no fear! That feeling of adrenaline running high, that fearlessness, allowed the author to create numerous flight-or-fight scenarios. Emotions helped clearly portray that character to you, the reader. The hero's feelings and actions got your heart pumping, too!

In our everyday life, most of us observe other people's emotions from a position of premature judgement. For example, we see and hear an individual bragging and have a negative thought about it or laugh disparagingly at them, actions which may both be based on preconceived notions.

Exercise 1: The Honest Observer

Try this 3-part exercise as a way to become a more neutral observer of other people's feelings and emotions, reactions and behaviors. Additionally, see what more you can learn about your own emotional reactions, thoughts and behaviors as you do the exercises.

Part A:

1.

Watch <u>media interviews</u>. They are a large part of our news programs. What is the underlying judgement or feeling the interviewer is communicating (is he or she really neutral and impartial)? What is the expressed feeling or emotion in the interviewee's responses? Just make a note; This is not about making those individuals right or wrong.

2.

Observe <u>public interactions amongst ordinary people</u>. This is also about watching strangers. You can do this at the shopping mall or at the bus stop. You can do this at restaurants or in business conferences when you yourself don't have to speak. Can you say there is a shared feeling or emotion among the people talking together? If so, just identify it. Can you say that one person is coming from a different feeling than the others in his comments or questions?

How are people reacting emotionally to each other during the conversation? Identify the specific feeling in each case and make a note of it. It's not about mocking them or judging them. It's not about making yourself feel superior or better than them in any way. Just observe and learn.

3.

When you have done this a few times, ask yourself, "How am I *just like them?"* Write down your honest answers!

Part B:

Although it is very tempting to pigeonhole an individual as "always angry" or "skeptical and negative", explore if that is really true as you observe other people you know.

1.

When you are sitting at a meal with others, or in a meeting during which you can be an attentive observer – choose one person to keep an eye on for a period of time. What is the range of emotions expressed by the individual?

2.

As you observe the person and note their feelings, watch for your own emotional reactions to them. What is your emotional response to a person seeming to tell a lie or suspiciously hesitating to provide information? To someone who is overtly bragging – and oblivious to doing so? Or to someone who is belittling or disapproving of another individual (whether that person is present or not)?

What you are doing here is observing your emotional relationship with other people you are somewhat familiar with. No one responds in exactly the same way when faced with a range of feelings. No one is always neutral.

3.

When you have done this a few times, ask yourself once more, "How am I *just like them?*" Jot down your honest answers!

Part C:

This exercise will focus on a close family member. More so than for friends and strangers, we tend to label our family members by their predominant emotional state. We say they are "serious" or "sensitive" or "happy" and so on.

1.

Your task is to focus on one family member for an extended period of time while doing a variety of activities with him or her. Don't hesitate to pull out your pocket notebook to note the emotions and feelings this person expresses while you are with them. Try to be a bit discreet, though!

2.

Is your label correct all the time? Do you notice any triggers to certain feelings in the individual? Do you purposely provide the trigger yourself – and if you do, state honestly why you do so! For instance, is it because it's "fun" to so easily stir up the other person?

Exercise 2: The Big Four In Action

List your four most prominent feelings on a small pocket-sized card. Take a look at the card throughout the day as a reminder. Observe yourself in interactive moments, as you bring these four most prominent feelings/reactions under your control.

Here are some ways of doing such an exercise. Adapt them to your own dominant feelings:

Part A: Interrupt Your Interrupting

How readily can you "kill" your urge to interrupt and state things you want to say? The urge to interrupt another individual in the course of a conversation is a behavior driven by feelings. Many of us, unfortunately, have this tendency.

Identify your own feelings attached to that urge to interrupt. In fact, an "urge" is itself a feeling! It is a lust, a craving, an itch to do something immediately. We say, "I _feel_ the urge to..." Perhaps, however — and let's be honest here — our personal feelings attached to the pressing need to interrupt comes more from pride and arrogance. We feel a prideful need to show off our greater intelligence or understanding of the subject at hand. Or we feel a need to belittle (a judgement from the energy of pride and criticism) those who are contributing to the conversation, because "they don't know what they're talking about".

Part B: Think Before Speaking

How quickly can you "bite your tongue" instead of saying something you'll regret as soon as the sound has left your mouth? This approach can be useful in many cases when you are better off observing others' feelings and behaviors than expressing your own.

When you have bitten your tongue, challenge yourself to identify feelings others are harboring or expressing (through word or body language). How can this help you connect with those individuals more empathically?

How hard will this be? Don't look at it as being as simple or difficult. Look at it as being simply a brand-new beneficial habit that you have decided with fierce determination to develop for yourself! Act as though you always think before speaking, and soon you will be doing so.

Will you perhaps feel frustrated when you have bitten your tongue, and are pausing to think and observe? Sure, because sometimes while you're doing that, the conversation veers off in a direction that doesn't allow you to interject your new thought! Let that be just fine. You don't need to control the conversation. You can be a neutral observer for a while, and no one will think that's strange.

Part C: Your Top Negative Reaction/Emotion

Go back to your emotional patterns and create a "change exercise" for yourself right here. Let's say, for instance, that your dominant pattern arises from feeling critical all the time. You feel chronically critical of people and situations; you just can't help yourself!

You never see the perfection, only the imperfections and failings. Fine, but how can you do what the EQ consultant did for the stage performer back in chapter 1? How can you turn that destructive emotional tendency to criticize every little thing upside-down? Identify the opposite, constructive feeling!

If your mind goes blank, just grab a dictionary! The opposite of feeling critical is feeling *appreciative, complimentary, approving, celebratory, or congratulatory, positive.*

How hard it would it be for you to turn your tendency to criticize into a tendency to express appreciation? To extend a compliment to an individual? To show approval as your first reflex? To act celebratory or extend congratulations? In other words, to just *act as if* you are feeling positively supportive, not only in the words you say, but in your facial and greater body language? Act as though doing the opposite is natural and easy to you, and eventually it will become so!

Exercise 3: Recognize Cause & Effect

You are now going to be observing the emotional effect that you have on other people. This may require some courage... or some humility!

Related to the prior exercise, if you are critical all the time, for instance, the emotional effect you have on others might manifest itself in a number of ways. They might just turn on their heel and walk away from you without another word. Or they suddenly burst into tears right in front of you. Or, they go on the counter-attack, finding some minute or major flaw of your own and throwing it right back in your face through some ugly verbal criticism that pours out of their mouth, as if they're just waiting for the opportunity.

Do you see what destructive emotional effect your own expression of negativity can create? A high-EQ leader would never behave in such a way!

For this exercise, be sure to actively observe the emotional effect you have on others. Do this when you are in meetings at work – as you speak during the meeting and immediately after having spoken, be watchful as you look at other participants' body language. Are they bored with what you have been saying? Are their bodies/faces tense with disagreement with your opinions? Are they fidgeting from impatience? Are they laughing at you – or with you? Just observe; don't get all puffed up by what you notice. But, likewise, don't collapse when you realize what their true reaction to you has been (8).

Do this at home, perhaps as you are trying to get children or family to do something on a tight schedule, or something they don't really want to do. Observe. Note.

In all cases, ask yourself, "How am I *just like them*? If this were done to me, would I react just as they do?" Be brutally honest with yourself. The others aren't wimps or losers (that is your negative emotional rationalization!) – they are just reacting to the buttons you have irresponsibly pushed. A high EQ individual doesn't push buttons for the fun of getting someone all stirred up. You never see it!

Chapter 5:

Your Life With Greater EQ

An emotionally aware individual doesn't rationalize or make excuses for his or her feelings. They do something about them! Aware individuals have observed the power of a single negative feeling to turn people away from them. Aware individuals understand the power of a single expressed negative emotion to cancel the business deal, to cancel personal dates with friends, to turn a new friendship or partnership permanently sour. Such emotionally intelligent, aware individuals have understood the power in being able to recognize and release such negative feelings, reactions, words and behaviors.

This is nothing more than true awareness – paying attention to one's surroundings and other people, and acting on the "data" one receives.

Working on continuously enhancing your emotional intelligence will have numerous immediate and cumulative effects, but perhaps the most life-changing aspect of having a high level of emotional intelligence is the <u>advanced self-awareness</u> which follows.

Developing an ever-sharper self-awareness is your key to living a different sort of life. A life that is more harmonious when you are with other people. A life that is more peaceful and quiet within your own being, whether you are on your own or with other people. A life in which you choose your feelings quite consciously, rather than (as before) allowing circumstances and other individuals to push those reactive emotional buttons without too much mindfulness from your side.

Self-awareness — as part of emotional intelligence — leads an individual to understanding which emotions are surging up, seeing what triggered them at the time, instantly seeing that the feeling is beneficial or detrimental in the given circumstances, activating the personal tools to let the feeling go or otherwise "manage" it – at the moment, by the mere decision to do so.

Being mindful of your own feelings is the best training for observing emotions and emotion-driven behavior in others.

As you practice *"emotionally intelligent mindfulness"* on yourself — as well as during your interactions with others — there is no doubt that you will begin to notice the benefits of greater attention to your own and other people's feelings. Your life as an emotionally self-aware person holds tremendous benefits not only for you, but also for all of the people with whom you regularly interact.

Immediate Effects

One of the immediate effects on working on your EQ is that you realize that all of us have an oversupply of feelings! One of the questions you may have about developing EQ is this: "How will I ever get to the end of all of my feelings, much less understand and influence those of other people?" Awareness of your feelings, in other words, shocks you into realizing just how many of them there are. You see just how all-pervasive they are in all your waking hours and activities, and in your sleep time, as well! You come to accept the fact that if you have so many feelings, so does everyone else!

Another effect on doing this work on yourself is the shocked realization of how much personal power you have been giving up by not becoming emotionally intelligent earlier in life. You see that you have not been calling on your personal power to the degree that you are able to. Mastery of your feelings and emotions gives you a great deal of control over how you approach life and its events, people, problems, goal-setting and goal-*getting*. A well-developed EQ gives you more power to direct events in your life according to your conscious choices. One might wonder why schools never teach this!

Another outcome of developing EQ that the majority of people notice quite soon, is how it reveals other personal strengths when they think they are only working on developing their "EQ muscles". You, too, might notice that your creativity soars, or that your creative focus lasts longer than it used to. You may notice that you are more solution-oriented than you used to be (you spin less in your mind on the problem).

You may also notice yourself rising out of your former shyness in social circumstances, or at times of interpersonal confrontation. Those circumstances and confrontations don't hold any real negative or scary power over you anymore, as your emotional strength allows you to step forward and say your piece with calm and confidence. You may notice that you wake up more frequently in a good mood – those pesky high/low mood swings are flattening and even disappearing...in favor of being in a happy state more naturally.

Cumulative Benefits

One of the first benefits you may comment upon weeks or months into this study is, "I have realized that it's just a feeling – not life or death." Related to this is the observation that, "A feeling is not forever. I have choices now!"

Another noticeable advantage of developing your EQ is that you've learned to identify your personal triggers. Over time, you have mastered how to defuse your impulsive, knee-jerk reactions to them. You'll notice a growing personal control over your own behaviors. By modifying or changing your feelings in a more positive direction, you recognize your behaviors have shifted. What used to be a strong trigger is being weakened, and a more appropriate behavior facilitated.

Again, this development of your emotional intelligence offers you more choices. For instance, if your trigger had been your teenager daughter's habit of rolling her eyes at every one of your comments, and your reaction had been to verbally express extreme irritation with her, you now have tools to make that an experience of the past. You can choose to be more neutral, or even just smile! Your EQ as regards others has trained you to see that she is just being rebellious to get attention or to express boredom, and now you know to handle that.

A third benefit that you may experience by setting aside destructive, unwanted or interfering feelings is an overall greater mental clarity. In personal, public or professional circumstances, you are better able to process both simple and complex situations more quickly through rational thinking. Your interfering feelings are no longer present to muddle your mind!

Another happy circumstance often resulting from ongoing development of EQ, is that you are much more comfortable in social settings that formerly bothered you. Nervousness, shyness, fear or panic can be resolved and dissolved before and during the event, through awareness of those emotional patterns. This type of emotion no longer dictates your interactions (or lack thereof) with other individuals. Striking up a conversation — even in socially manufactured types of settings — is turning out to be easier for you than before. In fact, you are finding yourself helping the wallflowers move out into the main room!

This comes from perceiving and evaluating emotional input and remembering that you have choices: You can react or you can act. You can fear what other people's judgements of you will be, or you can let that fear go and step up with courage. You can let circumstances crush you, or you can rise out of that feeling. You can then empathize and help others thrive instead of being crushed.

Developing your emotional intelligence leads you to experiencing more self-confidence and empowerment in group settings as well as with individuals who used to be difficult for you to get along with. You no longer feel pushed around or buffeted, bullied or pressured. Nor are you as fearful of negative commentary and judgements about you as you were before.

When someone previously tried to push your emotional buttons to get you to do something you didn't want to do, or pressure you to make changes that were not mutual, you felt out of control. EQ moves you into confidence and control. You can calmly fall back on rationality and reasoning to state your positions with courageousness. You no longer cave in to what the other person wants or expects of you when it is not in your self-interest (9).

As you can see, your life with greater personal self-awareness and a higher degree of emotional intelligence is more quiet and peaceful, which allows you to call on your power of clear thinking, courage and informed choice more easily.

Other People's Reactions

As you develop your EQ, others are going to react to you differently than they used to. Look at it this way: every emotion that we feel is an energy; we personally project the energy of that feeling out to our surroundings and to people nearby. In other words, if we feel fear, we communicate that fear to the people around us. We project out into the world an energy called fear that fills the space that we occupy.

You have probably entered a room and had the sense that the room "felt heavy" or "felt sad". That is because it does! Someone, or a group of people, was experiencing that emotional energy in that space before you entered the room. We are all sensitive to emotional energy!

As other individuals "feel" you differently, they will begin to adjust their own behaviors, reactions and words to rise to your level of energy. Since you have gone beyond developing just your personal EQ, you also can "feel" those individuals from a more positive, empathic and understanding perspective. Doesn't it help you get along better when both parties are in sync with the same positive energy? Young people today say, "I feel ya"; in the 60s and 70s young people used to say, "We're on the same vibration" or "The vibe is good" or "We're on the same wavelength".

There is something to be said for having high personal EQ that helps you in all interactions. It doesn't really matter whether the other individuals have a high or low EQ themselves; The person in the highest emotional energy will win the day.

What does this mean? Look at this situation:

You are coming from a feeling of non-judgement of the other party, from courageousness and enthusiasm (positive feelings), and you have a certainty about what must be done. The other party is coming from a feeling of irritation or vexation (both mild versions of negativity), mental confusion and fuzziness about what must be done

You will be the one that is successful at asserting your opinion, your position, your timetable, your process, your instructions and so on. You think clearly and see the solution. You see that the other party needs emotional support and you present your solution with compassion and ask if he or she thinks you have a good idea. You can do this and still feel good. The other one will bend with relief at your assertive clarity – because they are not pressured to come up with any new ideas – and do things your way, just because you have let them take the easy way out of an uncomfortable situation.

Why is it likely to be like this? Because the highest EQ energy always wins out! The higher energy from positive feelings brings clarity and ability to think on your feet. The lower energy and the mental confusion brought on by unwanted feelings prevents you from seeing and thinking clearly.

This is not to say that a high-EQ person will remain successful if he or she uses his abilities to manipulate other people in ways that are not mutual or transparent! However, people will usually gravitate towards emotionally intelligent individuals and seek out their companionship, their leadership or guidance, or their inspiration. They will want to bask in the influence and success of these natural leaders.

People instinctively lean towards the highest EQ individual present in times of conflicts or disagreement anywhere they occur (in the home, in the workplace, in public forums) because they have a sense that the high EQ individual is a clear thinker, a clear communicator, a quick study of situations, and thus a clear decision maker.

The high-EQ leader will be trusted and followed, even the most confusing times when no one actually has enough accurate information to make the best decisions. The high-EQ leader doesn't collapse under stress like others might – after all, what is stress but a messy collection of negative feelings? Masters of emotions know what to do with feelings – both their own and others'.

In Conclusion

Happiness is fleeting for most people. Far too many human beings cannot remember the last time they felt truly happy – carefree, confident, secure in their world. While further developing your EQ, you will discover that all that is in the way of your own happiness is... feelings! Feelings that are contrary to happiness. Negative feelings; Judgements that separate you from true rapport and relationship with others. With an improved emotional intelligence, and a few easy tools, you can let go of all the feelings – and the unwanted behaviors they lead to – and move into a space of <u>true happiness</u>.

Having a higher EQ will undoubtedly change your life. Remember: True happiness is you feeling more positive and lighthearted, whatever you are doing! That alone is more than enough reason to develop your emotional intelligence. And, by applying what we have learned in this book, you *will* get there. No more will you be swept away by the overwhelming current of your emotions. Instead, you'll be relaxed and in control while surfing the waves — finding joy in the moment as you keep your balance with ease.

In other words: You'll have achieved *emotional intelligence mastery*.

References

1) https://www.psychologytoday.com/basics/emotional-intelligence
Daniel Goleman's book, *Emotional intelligence,* 1995, Bantam Books
Daniel Goleman's e-book, *The Brain and Emotional intelligence: New Insights,* 2011

2) *Stern, William (1914) [1912 (Leipzig: J. A. Barth, original German edition)]. Die psychologischen Methoden der Intelligenzprüfung: und deren Anwendung an Schulkindern [The Psychological Methods of Testing Intelligence]*

3) http://www.inc.com/jessica-stillman/5-signs-you-have-a-high-eq.html

4) http://www.ozy.com/fast-forward/firms-make-hiring-emotional/33105

5) http://graduate.norwich.edu/resources-msl/infographics-msl/emotional-intelligence-eq-and-leadership/

6) http://www.alkpurusha.net/2013/09/amazing-story-mozambiques-meditating-president/

7) http://www.mindful.org/, http://www.apa.org/monitor/2012/07-08/ce-corner.aspx, https://www.psychologytoday.com/blog/compassion-matters/201303/benefits-mindfulness

8) Dr. Mark Goulston's book, "Just Listen: Discover the Secret to Getting Through to Absolutely Anyone", 2015, AMACOM

9) http://www.emotionalintelligencetraining.org.uk/benefits.html

CPSIA information can be obtained
at www.ICGtesting.com
Printed in the USA
LVOW08s1022031116
511507LV00010B/193/P